"The power of good questions
two men not only understand t
honed this skill over years of effective ministry. Steve and D_ _
excellent coaches because they have practiced the contents on a daily
basis. This is not a 'here go try this' book but rather 'we live this and it
works' book!"

Larry Barker, *Church Planting Director at BMAA*

"Powerful questions have shaped my life. They've been used of God to
deepen faith, enhance relationships and sharpen vision. I'm deeply
grateful to those who cared to ask.... Steve Ogne and Dave DeVries
have done a brilliant job compiling great questions for use in coaching
leaders. This book will be well-utilized in my ministry, and I trust, in
yours."

Dr. Dean Carlson, *President, One Challenge*

"*99 Powerful Questions for Christian Leaders* is a simple and practical
tool that keeps great questions right at your fingertips. By organizing
the questions according to common topics, this book allows you to
quickly flip to relevant questions for the area you're currently coaching.
You'll want to keep this book within arm's reach!"

Dr. Bob Logan, www.loganleadership.com

"*99 Powerful Questions for Christian Leaders* helps you listen to the
heart of the individual and helps you ask the right question at the right
time. This book flows out of Steve and Dave's own experience and is
an awesome little handbook for all your coaching appointments."

Mike Livingston, *Regional Director, Missionary Church Western Region*

"So often leaders don't stop to listen and learn before they love and lead. *99 Powerful Questions for Christian Leaders* will provide you with a foundation out of which to inspire, focus, encourage, challenge, motivate, and develop the leaders around you.... Don't miss out on increasing your leadership effectiveness by asking more powerful questions!"

Dr. Tom De Vries, *General Secretary, Reformed Church in America*

"It's been said that a picture is worth 1,000 words. For leaders who coach and empower others, a question can be the door to 1,000 answers.... These 99 questions are simple, but in their simplicity is their power. They get right to heart of things."

Dr. Tim Roehl, *Director of Training, One Mission Society (OMS)* Co-author, *"TransforMissional Coaching"* Author, *"Game Plan: Developing Intentional Missional Ministry"*

"For some time I've been a collector of good questions, and to some degree I've been able to effectively deploy a few of them.... Along the way I've had a question of my own: "Where are all the great questions hiding?" I think I've found the answer! ... My toolbox just got better."

Dr. Tom Nebel, *Speaker, Author, Coach, Provocateur* *www.tompnebel.com*

"Steve Ogne and Dave DeVries ... have excelled at coaching largely because they have asked the right questions at the right times - the revealing questions, the tough questions, the empowering questions, the self-discovery questions.... **99 Powerful Questions for Christian Leaders** equips coaches with an arsenal of well-placed questions.

Dr. Ken Priddy, *Executive Director - The GO Center*

"I was one of the guinea pigs for just about every leadership question in this book and it was a superb experience of leadership development.... Steve's coaching questions gave me an intentional track for changing my focus from leading to enabling others to lead. I have used these questions to help church planters become healthier and more effective leaders."

Dr. Jan D. Hettinga, *Founder of the Northsound Church Planting Network, Seattle, WA, Author of Follow Me: Experience the Loving Leadership of Jesus*

"Most people do their best thinking in the presence of a powerful question. Steve Ogne and Dave DeVries have given us an excellent resource for creating such an environment.... I look forward to using these questions and creating the space for deeper reflection and awareness. I am also excited to watch these questions do their work and seeing the many aha moments that result from using them."

Kevin Stebbings, *Leadership Coach and Trainer*

"As someone who has been actively coaching leaders for the last 20 years I am grateful to Dave and Steve for placing top-notch questions all in one place. As I read through the categories and the questions I found myself saying... "Now, that's a great question!", or "I need to start asking that question!" This book will advance anyone who wants to get better at asking questions. I look forward to recommending this book to as many leaders as I can."

Buck Rogers, *President, Empower Clarity* (Coaching, Consulting, Lifeplanning)

Other books by Steve Ogne

The Church Planter's Toolkit (co-authored with Bob Logan)

Churches Planting Churches (co-authored with Bob Logan)

Empowering Leaders through Coaching (co-authored with Tom Nebel)

Transformissional Coaching (co-authored with Tim Roehl)

The Leadership Ladder (co-authored with Ken Priddy)

Other books by Dave DeVries

Six-Word Lessons to Discover Missional Living

The Missional Journey (co-authored with Bob Logan)

99 Powerful Questions™

for

Christian Leaders

Questions to Coach

Christian Leaders toward Greater Effectiveness

and How to Use Them

Steve Ogne

and

Dave DeVries

Foreword by Keith E. Webb

99 POWERFUL QUESTIONS®
LEVERAGE YOUR CREDIBILITY

99 Powerful Questions™ for Christian Leaders

Published by 99 Powerful Questions Publishing
A division of Personalized, Custom Publishing Inc.
2707 Gordon Street
Raleigh NC 27608
www.99PowerfulQuestions.com

Cover by: Elijah Hankins
Edited by: Deborah Howell

ISBN: 978-1-942601-02-9

Printed in the United States of America
First edition 2015

Contents

Foreword by Keith Webb   ix

Introduction   xi

Listen Actively   1

Celebrate Wins   11

Care Personally   21

Strategize Plans   29

Evangelizing and Discipling Skills   39

Family Issues and Relationships   47

Interpersonal Relationships and Resistance   55

Listening Skills Development   61

Mobilizing Leaders and Volunteers   67

Prayer and Spiritual Disciplines   77

Time Management   83

Vision and Planning   91

Develop Character and Leadership   99

Challenge Specifically   113

Acknowledgements   121

Foreword

Questions have the ability to send people on a journey—a quest. It's a journey of discovery. Rather than guiding people by telling them what *we* think, we can ask questions and explore *their* thinking.

Many times we explore familiar territory. However, there are those special times, those magical moments, when a question generates a sudden shift in perspective that gives us new eyes with which to see the world around us. That's a powerful question!

Powerful questions are those that reveal information—perspectives, motivations, and ideas—for the other person. It's in thinking about and responding to a question that we become clearer on something that may be fuzzy in our minds.

99 Powerful Questions for Christian Leaders is loaded with excellent questions. For example, what if you asked me this question:

> Q6 What issues are important to you right now?

To answer, I must think about the various issues I face and prioritize them. We could go deeper by discussing how I determine what is important right now. This discussion would reveal my motivations, fears, values, and priorities.

Discussing priorities at this depth can cause a radical shift in thinking.

Questions can also prompt me to think about areas of my life or ministry I haven't been paying attention to. If you tell me to pay attention to them, I may become defensive. But if you ask me about them, you cause me to wonder ... and that's powerful.

Take this question:

Q92 What do your leaders need from you?

I haven't been thinking about what my leaders need from me. I've been thinking about what I need them to do. This question causes me to reflect on how well I am helping my leaders, and what I need to provide so that they will be more successful. In one question my orientation has moved from seeing my leaders as a problem to seeing my own actions as part of the solution.

Dave DeVries and I first learned to coach from Steve Ogne. He's a master at asking powerful questions. I'm happy to recommend their book to you so you will be better equipped to support the Christian leaders around you.

Dr. Keith E. Webb
Author of *The COACH Model for Christian Leaders*

Introduction

Powerful questions have an amazing impact. Whether you ask yourself a powerful question or you ask another person, the right question in the right moment can provide new perspectives and direction.

Author John Whitmore discovered that "telling or asking closed questions saves people from having to think. Asking open questions causes them to think for themselves." We want to help you to ask better questions. When you are developing leaders around you, asking questions that cause deeper self-reflection will lead to powerful insights and actions.

Powerful questions will keep you from talking too much. They also value the leader you are investing in. When you are asking questions that relate to the leader, you remind the leader that the conversation is about him or her, not about you.

When a leader is engaged in responding to powerful questions, it keeps him or her actively participating in personal development. Just shutting your mouth and allowing a leader to respond specifically to a powerful question can accelerate forward progress.

The 99 powerful questions in this short book are not meant to be exhaustive—you'll want to develop hundreds more.

This list is a starting point to help you ask the type of questions that lead to the self-discovery and accompanying accountability that best serve the leader.

Often we have been asked, "What makes a question powerful?" We have found that the most powerful questions are those that cause personal self-reflection and discovery. Rather than telling a leader what to do (which may seem obvious to you), powerful questions help a leader see for him- or herself what is effective and empowering.

Powerful questions are intentional, not random. Realize that questions can be used, misused, or abused. They can be used to help the leader or to harm the leader. They have a clear purpose. They will surface information, increase awareness, or promote action. You'll find all three of these kinds of questions in *99 Powerful Questions for Christian Leaders*.

Yet, we don't just provide a list of questions; we show you how to use them. Each question can be asked of yourself or to empower another leader. Here are the categories we've included:

- Listen Actively
- Celebrate Wins
- Care Personally
- Strategize Plans
- Evangelizing and Discipling Skills

- Family Issues and Relationships
- Interpersonal Relationships and Resistance
- Listening Skills Development
- Mobilizing Leaders and Volunteers
- Prayer and Spiritual Disciplines
- Time Management
- Vision and Planning
- Develop Character and Leadership
- Challenge Specifically

It's our hope that this simple book will help you develop the practice of asking powerful questions. Here are a few principles to remember:

- Powerful questions are easily understood.
- Powerful questions encourage thoughtful reflection.
- Powerful questions are open-ended.
- Powerful questions enable self-disclosure.

Because we value and believe in the leaders we are empowering, the questions we ask are to expand and elevate their identity and ability. The questions are intended to lead the leader to his or her own discovery, not ours.

We believe powerful questions are the best tool for empowering Christian leaders. Use them wisely.

Dr. Steve Ogne
Somis, California

Dr. Dave DeVries
Bellevue, Washington

Listen

Actively

Q1

How is your ministry?

Always start coaching conversastions with a very generic, open-ended question that allows the leader to set the tone of the conversation.

A general observation of how things are going is helpful in framing the dialogue. A quick evaluation of "thumbs up" or "thumbs down" can also pinpoint which areas of ministry require more attention.

Q2

How are you personally?

It is essential to have a pulse on what's happening in both ministry and personal life.

One time I jumped straight to a ministry question, and at the end of the call the guy said, "By the way—my wife and I split up last night." Wow!

Always check in on different levels. You usually have to press ministry people to talk about how they are doing personally. They easily revert back to ministry. Keep pressing in.

Q3

How is your family?
Your spouse?

Start broadening the context out. It is important to check in on a leader's family and spouse. Consider two directions: "What's good? What's not?" Give equal opportunity to share joys and concerns.

Related to their spouse, you can say, "Tell me about your last night out together." Discover when it was and how it went. If it was too long ago, go after that.

Q4

Tell me about last week's meeting.

This question can be modified to focus on any form of meeting: small group, Sunday gathering, leadership meeting, etc.

The goal here is to have a current context for what's happening. Whether it was good or bad, you want to know at the beginning of a coaching conversation. This could potentially shape the whole conversation going forward.

Q5

How are you and God doing?

This is my favorite question for taking a spiritual temperature. It's less intimidating than asking, "How was your quiet time?"

They can respond in multiple ways—thanksgiving, struggle, etc. This gives a glimpse of their spiritual context.

Q6

What issues are important to you right now?

This is a focusing question. Here you are actually beginning to clarify the outcome of the coaching conversation.

The key thing we've learned is that we need to get multiple issues on the table before we determine what's most important to talk about first.

Discover three to five issues. One is not enough.

Q7

What concerns you right now?

This question has some urgency to it. You want to discover more than just the challenges ahead.

When I ask this question, I'm exploring a deeper level of awareness that surfaces an emotional response of concern, anxiety, or stress. Every leader will need to address these concerns at some point.

Q8

Where are you feeling resistance?

As I listen, when I am sensing resistance in the conversation, I'll often ask a leader where they are feeling resistance.

You can also ask more directly: "Why are you feeling defensive?" Identifying the sources of resistance can generate options. You can then coach them forward.

Celebrate

Wins

Q9

What are you excited about?

Starting here creates a positive tone for coaching conversation. Ask the person you are coaching to focus on what is happening and what they are excited about.

This question allows you to move forward from a positive posture. Next, discern whether they are excited about the right stuff. Their answer will tell you where their head may be at.

Q10

What was your greatest accomplishment this month?

This question is about confidence and affirmation. By reviewing what's been accomplished, you build them up. I want to know that they accomplished something since we last met.

This is also a time to reflect on other action steps or assignments from the last conversation. If they don't bring them up, I will.

Q11

What prayers have been answered?

It's easy to focus on what you are asking God to do. Make sure you take time to reflect on what God has already done and to thank Him.

Invite leaders to consider how to keep track of all the ways God is answering prayers.

Q12

Where is God working in your ministry?

This is the opposite of asking, "How are you working?" This question helps in getting one's eyes on God in the midst of all of the ministry activity they are doing.

Too often, ministry leaders can forget whose ministry it really is. Focusing on the activity of God and what He is accomplishing will bring clarity.

Q13

How has God been faithful?

"The steadfast love of the Lord never ceases; his mercies never come to an end; they are new every morning; great is your faithfulness" (Lamentations 3:22–23 ESV).

It's easy to lose heart in the midst of church ministry. Leaders face challenges constantly. Yet God is faithful. Take time to remember His faithfulness.

This question brings encouragement.

Q14

What milestones have been accomplished?

This question can be used in two ways:

> 1) to measure ministry effectiveness (whether the leader is doing anything, and if so, what).

> 2) to track progress over a series of coaching conversations, or just the past month. It's a good review question.

Even when there has not been much accomplished, this focuses on what has actually been accomplished.

Q15

Where have you demonstrated your best leadership?

Here the focus is on building leaders up in their confidence. If they can articulate when they demonstrated solid leadership recently, they will be more likely to repeat this.

Affirming specific leadership behaviors will raise their self-awareness and reinforce their leadership skill.

Q16

Who are your most loyal ministry partners?

It's easy for leaders to feel alone and isolated. Help them focus on who is partnering with them.

You can expand this area by asking, "Who else do you need to be celebrating with?" "How are you celebrating with those people?" "How have you shown appreciation to them?

Care

Personally

21

Q17

What concerns do you or your spouse have about your ministry?

This is a transitioning question from ministry to personal care. It introduces concerns on the ministry side followed up on the personal side.

Some people will go there easily; others will require asking three times to get them to open up on a personal level. They may only be willing to talk about ministry and surface stuff. Try to uncover the spouse's concerns, as they are usually more insightful.

Q18

What can I be praying with you about?

Prayer is one of the most effective ways to demonstrate care inside a coaching conversation. Praying together communicates that you care personally for the leader you are coaching.

When you stop and pray, essentially you are saying, "I heard you, and your need is important enough to talk to God about right now."

Praying also reminds a leader that God cares!

Q19

What help do you need?

Help the person you are coaching to identify specifically what help they need. This is an important step before determining who can help them.

It's easy to feel overwhelmed and get stuck in a thinking pattern that doesn't access helpful resources. This question moves a person to consider what external help is necessary.

Q20

Where do you receive support and encouragement?

Once the help needed is identified, a leader can begin to consider who is available to help.

Be careful not to insert yourself into the question by asking, "What support or encouragement do you need *from me*?" Instead, help them explore their existing support network. The coach isn't there to meet needs, but rather to make connections to get needs met.

Q21

How do you feel when you get resistance?

All leaders face resistance at some point in their leadership journey.

This is a great "feeling" question. It helps put leaders in touch with their emotions. When they address their feelings, they can get a better response to the resistance.

By asking about feelings, you can identify potential defensiveness and coach toward a more positive response.

Q22

What have you done for fun lately?

Relating holistically, most people are working too hard and may likely need a break in the action. You can help a leader to identify the need for recreation, release, and revitalization—and to plan accordingly.

This question can also be a great way to relieve pressure in a conversation, to allow space to take a breath and transition to a positive note in a heavy conversation.

Q23

How well are you sleeping?

Often fatigue is an issue that adds to the stress that a leader faces.

Caring personally for the leader's physical, spiritual, emotional, and relational well-being is empowering. Too often, few others in a leader's life will ask this kind of question.

It may also be helpful to ask, "Are you sleeping enough?" or "What adjustments need to be made to improve your sleep?"

Strategize

Plans

Q24

How comfortable and confident are you with your vision, values, and mission?

Before developing strategy, reconnect to the leader's vision. This requires that they reflect on their vision, values, and mission.

This question can be a reality check to discern issues related to alignment and mission drift.

Q25

What is your strategic plan for implementation?

"Begin with the end in mind" is a familiar axiom. Take time to help the leader reflect on where they are, where they are going, and how they are going to get there.

This is critical to strategic development. People don't just need to hear about vision—they need to know how that vision will become reality.

Q26

What are your immediate priorities?

Coaching conversations provide focus on what's important and what's urgent. These aren't always the same.

As noted in Stephen Covey's classic *The 7 Habits of Highly Effective People*, it's often the nonurgent yet important activities that are ignored.

Help the leader identify those things that need to be given their attention first.

Q27

How are you continuing to attract and involve new people?

This is a good gathering and assimilation question. It applies to leaders across the board, not just to church planters.

There has to be a constant flow of new people for ministry to continue to grow and expand. Leaders cannot just focus on shepherding those people they already have.

Q28

What is your vision for multiplication?

Think about multiple generations. Don't just be focused on growing your gathering. Focus on expanding God's kingdom through multiplying disciples, leaders, and churches. How many churches might be started in the next five years?

Q29

Have you developed a ministry flowchart? Is it realistic? Working?

Any of these can become a longer conversation with follow-up questions. These are entry questions regarding strategy and plans.

A good ministry flowchart involves all the primary ministry opportunities and demonstrates movement from one to another.

Q30

How are evangelism and spiritual growth happening?

Connecting evangelism and spiritual growth forces the leader to start at the beginning. For every ministry, the weakest areas are evangelism and leadership development.

Q31

How is leadership development happening?

This surfaces things that often get dropped off the plate.

The church only grows on the edges. The front edge is evangelism, the back edge is leadership development. Most pastors spend time trying to fix the middle.

Q32

What ministry systems do you need?

A system is anything done routinely and repeatedly. Entry systems, follow-up, assessment—it's more cool to refer to them as rhythms these days rather than systems. A system for each—get them to unpack what they need for spiritual formation, community, and mission. Then over time focus on how the systems are working: red light, yellow light, or green light for each system.

Evangelizing and Discipling Skills

Q33

With how many unchurched families do you have contact?

This is a missional question, no matter to whom you are talking. It's about personal missionality. Without contact, there is no mission. This question often exposes a need for intentionality in a leader's life.

Q34

How does your life have integrity with unchurched people?

That's a deep one—the initial response is often "What do you mean?"

Mission's coach, Phil Graf, adds, "Is your life spicy to unchurched people? Is it attractive to unchurched people?"

Q35

Who have you baptized recently?

This works in any context, focusing on measurement. It is important to help leaders stay focused on the right thing, the main thing.

Q36

How are new believers being incorporated into your ministry?

Look for stories. Ask the leader to give three specific examples of how they have done this. Don't assume.

Q37

What are you doing to make disciples?

It's not everything. If the response is "everything," there's probably nothing being done.

What are the specific things you are doing to bring people across the line of faith? And, what are the specific things you are doing to help people follow Jesus?

Q38

What kind of time have you spent with anyone who is a non-Christian this past month?

How much time? What did they do? In most instances, they may have spent a couple of fifteen-minute windows. Conversations. Brief.

Follow up—identify the total time, then focus on how much time it would take to create a relationship that would support the hearing of the Gospel.

What would it look like to spend at least a tithe of your ministry time with lost people?

Family Issues and Relationships

Q39

Do others see you as self-reliant or dependent upon God?

This has a lot to do with spiritual development as well.

Often we don't think about how others perceive us. This question is useful to get leaders to look at themselves through the eyes of others—specifically as it relates to their dependence on God or lack thereof.

Excellent follow-up question: How do you demonstrate dependence on God?

Q40

How would you like to grow spiritually?

We all would say that we would like to grow spiritually, but very rarely do we have a plan to make this reality. A simple question like this will help a leader begin to formulate a plan for spiritual formation.

Q41

How are your family's spiritual needs being met?

Some of the most spiritually neglected people are the spiritual leader's family. It's always important to ask how the leader's family's spiritual needs are being met. This will help them to identify or increase their effectiveness in being a spiritual leader at home.

Q42

How are each of your family members getting enough of your time and attention?

Family spiritual leadership takes time. Are each of them getting enough time and attention? Do you have dates with individual family members? Do you have a regular family night?

It always takes intentionality.

Q43

When do you regularly take time off with your spouse?

Pretty straightforward. Always encourage leaders to have quality time with their spouse. Do they plan for weekly dating, monthly overnight, and annual vacation? This needs to be intentional.

The thrust of this question is to get out the calendar and mark it down. It's very useful after a successful season, or a difficult season, to relax and rebuild at home.

Q44

How is the balance of family and ministry going?

Another way to ask: There are seven nights in a week—how many of them are you home? The goal is to be home the majority of nights to ensure that the family is getting the majority of time and focus.

Q45

How often do you give your spouse a day off?

We talk about the value of the Sabbath for a pastor—but what about the spouse? Because of employment and responsibilities with children, it may take extra intentionality. Your spouse needs time off from you and from responsibility.

Interpersonal Relationships and Resistance

Q46

Where do you sense resistance in your leadership or group?

Leaders often face resistance. It's important to recognize it and address it. It's likely coming from a particular individual.

Failure to address the resistance often creates an emotional and spiritual drain on a leader.

Q47

What are the surfacing issues and underlying values involved?

Now—what are they resisting?

It could be the vision, a program, teaching, etc. There could be any number of areas of resistance. Take the time to clarify it. This step is necessary before addressing it.

Q48

How do you respond to resistance?

Figure out how to respond in a nondefensive manner. What would that look like?

Q49

Are there any unresolved conflicts in your circle of leadership right now?

Unresolved conflicts in social, ministry, and family circles are a constantly available tool of the devil to disrupt ministy. Checking in to assess areas of potential conflict is a preventive action.

If there is an excessive number of unresolved conflicts, it may indicate some areas of character development that need to be addressed.

Q50

When was the last time you spent time with a good friend (besides your spouse)?

Paying attention to our own personal relationships is important, especially outside of ministry circles.

You could follow up with: What did you do? How did that impact you and/or encourage you?

Listening Skills Development

Q51

How and when do you listen to unchurched people?

Ministry leaders spend most of their time listening to Christians, and that begins to shape the way they think and relate to people. It's necessary to listen to unchurched people so that you have a broader perspective on ministering to people. This may include naive listening to those around you, or intentionally having conversations with unchurched people. This will increase your understanding and ability to relate in meaningful ways to unbelievers.

Q52

How and when do you listen to God?

We all have a prayer time. Generally when we pray we do most of the talking. The real question here is when do you shut up and listen to God? When, where, and how do you do this?

Q53

How and when do you listen to your spouse? Your children?

You have dinnertime to focus in and hear what's happening. When else?

When do you listen to their world? Often dinner isn't available as a family. You need to identify other times to listen to your spouse and others.

Q54

How and when do you listen to leaders?

Most of the time leaders pay other leaders to talk, not often taking the opportunity to listen to them. One of the best gifts we can offer leaders is to listen to them—ministry concerns or success, stress in life, personal issues. It's a good idea to build listening opportunities into team meetings. Practice listening more.

Q55

How can you improve your listening skills?

Most of us are too busy talking to listen well—we need to work on being quiet. Asking questions is a great way to work on this. If you ask a question, you have to at least be polite enough to listen to the answer.

Mobilizing Leaders and Volunteers

Q56

How do you encourage and motivate volunteers?

Most of us are anxious to recruit and empower volunteers and put them to work. Then we tend to drop the ball and fail to follow through on appropriate ancouragement. Appreciation, motivation, recognition, and celebration are all important.

Brainstorm ten ways to motivate volunteers. Get out of the box of doing it the same way all the time. It becomes much more personal and meaningful.

Q57

How have you practiced good coaching?

Coaching is a great way to encourage and mobilize volunteers. Listen actively. Ask powerful questions. Help others discover how God wants them to move forward.

Q58

What position descriptions for key leaders and volunteers have you created?

Written descriptions provide clear assignments and accountability for any position. This gives people more confidence because they know specifically what they are being asked to do and are more likely to take the assignment.

Q59

How and when are you casting vision for leaders?

We all know that vision is forgotten very quickly, so we need to routinely cast vision for leaders.

We want to cast a high-level vision that connects a volunteer's ministry assignment to the mission of the church. Recruit nursery workers not to babysit, or change diapers, but to help parents worship God. Or youth workers not to hang out with students, but to disciple students.

Q60

How will you begin an apprenticing system?

Apprenticing includes "you watch me–we do it together–I watch you." This is the easiest training available—it requires no extra meetings. It can apply to all levels: ushers apprenticing ushers, elders apprenticing elders, pastors apprenticing pastors. The best way to get started apprenticing is to jump in. Identify one to three people you can begin with now—in your small group, in your mission team—and begin by taking them with you on assignments.

Q61

How will you appreciate and encourage volunteers this month?

Christian leaders are always working with volunteers. Recruiting, training, coaching—these activitities can become all-consuming.

Yet it's important for a leader to provide appreciation and encouragement in tangible ways. Consider brainstorming a list of ten ways, and pick one or two specific ways to implement each month.

Q62

How will you find the leaders you need?

Every leader says that they are looking for leaders, but often they aren't really looking. Develop clear descriptions of what you are looking for, and invite others to recruit with you.

Individually go after people—don't just make announcements. Give people the opportunity to pray and respond. Asking everyone is asking no one. Asking two people will get two responses. One of them may be yes.

Q63

How will you identify and raise up leaders?

Most of the time, pastors and church planters are not intentional enough about their leadership development. They want help, yet they don't know what kind of leaders they need. And they haven't asked anybody.

You have to identify the specific need. What kind of leaders do you need? What do you need them to do? Establish the opportunity, make the ask— then you can develop them up. Consider a holistic development process.

Q64

What leaders do you have?
What leaders do you need?

It's often said that everything rises and falls on leadership. Start by empowering the leaders that God has given to you. Invest in their development. Train them. Coach them. Pray with them and for them. Release ministry responsibility to them. Love them.

Prayer and Spiritual Disciplines

Q65

What kind of personal intercessory prayer team do you have?

I generally ask this question because most volunteer leaders don't have anyone—and many professionals have too few or an outdated and neglected prayer team. This makes them susceptible because they are doing without protection. Spiritual warfare is more intense than ever before. We need to be more aggressive to get this prayer covering in place for our own sake, our family's sake—and the ministry's sake.

Q66

What have you read in the Bible this past week?

This is a way to check in on a leader's self-feeding behaviors. If coaching a pastor, I ask specifically about reading apart from sermon prep.

Follow-up question: How has that changed your life or behavior?

If they can't answer right away, it could be indicative of an issue that needs to be addressed.

Q67

Where do you find yourself currently resisting God?

This is actually one of my favorite questions—it always provokes a response. Most of us don't think about this. When we can identify issues of resistance or neglect, verbalizing them can give opportunity to change or improve behaviors. If no one asks, we will just keep doing what we are doing—which can be dangerous.

Q68

What specific things are you praying for?

I generally don't ask, "Are you praying?"—but rather ask, "What are you praying for?" The content of their prayer tells me a lot about them and their ministry. If it's just for themselves, I'm concerned. What they are praying for their church will tell me a lot about them as a pastor.

Most often I want to check and see if they are praying for any lost people by name.

Time

Management

Q69

How many hours are you giving to ministry?

This is an open-ended question designed to identify those who might be overworking as well as those who might be slacking. Very few people are right on target. Almost everyone is overdoing or underdoing it.

One coaching tool is time tracking for a week (by the hour or half day, with morning, afternoon, evening). Ask rather than judge: Is it too much or too little?

Q70

What tasks that you are currently doing will you give to volunteers?

With church planters, it's almost always volunteers. What tasks are burning time? Burning energy? Not in your gift mix?

Q71

Tell me about your rest and recreation plan.

If working too much, they are not resting enough. People in ministy, volunteer and professional, need to protect their personal Sabbath, and it may not be on Sunday. A Jewish Sabbath is twenty-four hours, not eight hours. Sabbath time can also include an annual vacation period, a weekly family night, or a weekly day off.

Q72

For what do you wish you had more time?

Often the first response is either work or family. Press them on what they need time for themselves: hobby, exercise, rest (not just more time for sermon prep).

Q73

What personal and time management tools or techniques do you use?

This question finds out what calendar and tools they are using. How's that working for you? Identify what's broken. In addition to calendar, consider social media—are they a time burner? Are they helping you in ministry?

Q74

How and when do you say no?

Follow up—what was the last ministry thing you said no to? What was the last family thing you said no to? Which do you say no to more often?

Vision
and
Planning

Q75

How do you seek vision from God?

And when? Part of the Sabbath ritual from Q71 above (vacation or day off or monthly day away) is intentional opportunities to have extended time of prayer and reflection to seek vision from God.

Secondly, keep eyes on community to see what God sees and keep that in focus.

Thirdly, share vision with others—and they share vision with you. (Iron sharpens iron.)

Q76

How do you communicate vision and values to others?

And when? Some categories: Visually? Verbally? In print? In action? Some have said that vision is lost in thirty days. This means we need to cast vision until we are sick of it—that's about the time our people are starting to get it. Almost everybody underarticulates vision, in terms of frequency, detail, or clarity.

Q77

Share with me your mission statement.

Vision is the broad strokes of what we believe God is going to accomplish. Mission is the specific way we are going to achieve the vision (how we get there)—the focus of your whole ministry in a sentence. You might also want to consider using a description of God's unique assignment for your ministry or church.

Q78

How empowering is your mission statement?

A good mission statement will include whom you are trying to reach, how you are going to reach them, and what the result is going to be.

It will describe what a leader is compelled to do. It will have an energizing impact on the leader.

Q79

How have you approached planning in the past?

The goal here is to pull out of them anything they have ever used in terms of intentional planning. It can be helpful to ask: What worked? What didn't work? What was missing? What was confusing?

Q80

What planning tools have you found to be helpful?

Calendars, goal setting, surveys—the vision/mission itself should always be the guiding factor on reality checks for our plans.

If you do this plan, how will it accomplish the mission?

Q81

When and how will you involve your team in a planning process?

Planning can involve your small group, your staff— you can initiate planning retreats. None of those will happen unless you are intentional about it. Try to avoid mountaintop planning: going to the mountain to make a plan by yourself, and then coming back to convince everybody.

Develop Character and Leadership

Q82

What is one non-ministry area where God is asking you to grow?

Most often our coaching is ministry focused, but we have a responsibility to encourage personal growth as well. You might ask this question to identify where God is already working in a person so that you can encourage them. You are not trying to create another agenda for their lives or discourage them. Not, "I think you should focus on your marriage." Instead, "What's one area that God wants you to work on in your marriage?" Then you can help coach them forward rather than being a "bad guy."

Q83

What are the specific tasks right now that you consider incomplete?

This is an inventory tool to allow the leader to identify tasks that need to be done or are incomplete. Logical follow-up: Which of these are most important? Which can you delegate or just never do? What do you need to do this week? Take inventory, then prioritize.

Deeper level: You can also use this question to evaluate whether people are focused on the right things, like developing leaders versus maintaining ministry.

Q84

What have you read in the secular press this week?

Cultural awareness is more important than ever in our postmodern society. We need to know what's going on around us. Those who follow us most closely need to know that we are aware of circumstances and trends that are going on around us. The best way to achieve that is to read one secular book (nonfiction) a month and subscribe to one secular newsmagazine.

Q85

What would your spouse tell me about your energy level, spirit, and state of mind?

This question is designed to provoke a deeper level of honesty about emotions and feelings. Sometimes you need to ask the spouse, preferably in the presence of the leader.

Q86

How might Satan try to invalidate you as a person or as a servant of the Lord?

When Satan wants to disable or disrupt ministry, he most often goes for the weakest link. How does Satan attack you or go after you in your weakest area? How can you increase your spiritual protection in that area (including prayer and accountability partners)?

Q87

How is your sexual perspective? Tempted? Dealing with fantasies? Entertainment?

How and when are you the most tempted sexually? It's important to give leaders (male or female) an opportunity to reflect and be accountable for their sexual behavior and thought lives. Use a variety of questions in this area, and don't be afraid to be direct.

Q88

Where are you financially right now? Under control? Under anxiety? In great debt?

Three biggies for character: money, sex, and power. It's important to help leaders honestly evaluate and address their financial circumstances. This includes the opportunity to describe what is or is not happening, as well as to intentionalize planning and communication. This is also a great opportunity for prayer (and possibly celebration).

Q89

What would you say are your fears at the present time?

If Satan is not attacking our person, sex life, or finances, he's disabling our leadership with fear. And if not in the church, it's often in the home.

Giving any fear a name is the first step to being able to address it and overcome it. If you just go around fearful all the time, you are stuck. If you can name it, then you can address it. The devil uses our fears to disable ministry.

Q90

What are your greatest confusions about your relationship with God?

Sometimes we are so busy working for God that we neglect our relationship with Him or get a twisted idea of His nature and character. So the question here has to do with our spiritual identity, sense of calling, or even our sense of self-worth.

Q91

How would you describe your leadership style?

Pretty straightforward question. Follow up: What kind of leadership or personality surveys have you used? What do they say about you? What would your teammates say about your leadership style? Ultimately, what needs to change in order to be more effective?

Q92

What do your leaders need from you?

Most people in ministry spend time thinking about what they need from their leaders, not thinking about what their leaders need from them. Brainstorm a list of leaders' needs that you and only you can provide to them.

Q93

Who are you personally mentoring?

Most people are recruiting and using leaders rather than developing or mentoring leaders. How are you doing this? How much time are you giving to this in a given week? How are you developing your mentoring skills?

Challenge

Specifically

Q94

What are your
next steps?

This is a simple question designed to help leaders make a decision related to their actions—and then to prioritize their action steps.

It's helpful not to just focus on a single next step. If this action is blocked, they won't make any progress toward their goal. Focus on identifying the next three steps (as a minimum).

Q95

What are you believing God for?

This question is designed to increase their faith as they set goals or make action plans.

It's important to consider our part in moving forward as well as God's part in accomplishing the results. Exploring a leader's level of faith and what they are anticipating God will do is helpful in the pursuit of any goal or objective.

Q96

When will you seek vision from God (calendar)?

This question is coming back around to time management, to help a leader prioritize vision and goal setting into their planning process.

Jesus often spent time alone with God to discern future direction. Encourage leaders to seek time alone with God to hear from God and to discern His direction for their future.

Q97

What are your highest priorities for this month?

This question is designed to create laser focus on the actions or activities that will have the greatest impact on the most important goals.

Often we ask, "What's the one thing you could do that would make everything else easier or unnecessary?" (from Gary Keller, *The One Thing*).

Q98

When and how will you take time for planning?

We've all heard it said: "If you fail to plan, you plan to fail." Asking "when" will help a leader to get the next planning session into their schedule. Asking "how" will help a leader identify the process that will work best for planning.

Focus on both "when" and "how."

Q99

What will you do to encourage the spiritual life of your group?

Often we are so anxious to get things done that we neglect the spiritual process and/or the spiritual needs of the group. How will you be both their pastor and their leader?

See the entire

99 Powerful Questions Series
at *99powerfulquestions.com*

Learn more about Steve Ogne
at steveogne.org

Learn more about Dave DeVries
at davedevries.org

Acknowledgments

The idea for this book was birthed a few years ago based on the asking hundreds of powerful questions as we've worked with church planters. The first compilation of 99 questions appeared in Empowering Leaders Through Coaching (1995). Together, we began to dialogue on our thinking process as we would ask these questions and this resulted in the book you have today.

We have been blessed to partner together in brining this project to life. We couldn't have done it without the support of many others:

To our amazing editors, Debbie Howell, Rachael Grotte and Alison McConnaughey - you've made this book so much easier to read.

To My Graphics Geek, Elijah Hankins - thanks for covering the book and helping us look so good.

To our 99 Powerful Questions team, Brandon Lee and Steve Swayne - we are grateful for your belief in this project and look forward to seeing many more 99PQ books to come.

To Deanne DeVries and Jane Ogne - we appreciate your ongoing love, support, encouragement, patience, and cheerleading along the way!

Made in the USA
Middletown, DE
11 July 2015